STARTING TECHNO[...]

AIR

John Williams

Illustrated by
Malcolm S. Walker

Wayland

STARTING TECHNOLOGY

Titles in this series

AIR
TIME
WATER
WHEELS

Words printed in **bold** appear in the glossary on page 30

First published in 1990 by
Wayland (Publishers) Ltd
61 Western Road, Hove
East Sussex BN3 1JD, England

This edition published in 1991 by
Wayland (Publishers) Ltd

Editor: Anna Girling
Designer: Kudos Design Services

British Library Cataloguing in Publication Data
Williams, John
Air.
1. Air
I. Title II. Series
551.51

ISBN 1 85210 983 1 Hardback
ISBN 0 7502 0268 8 Paperback

Typeset by Kudos Editorial and Design Services, Sussex, England
Printed in Italy by Rotolito Lombarda S.p.A.
Bound in Belgium by Casterman S.A.

CONTENTS

Air is Everywhere 4
Windmills 6
Hand Windmills 8
Wind Wheels 10
Wind Force 12
More Measuring 14
Kites 16
Hot-Air Balloons 18
Parachutes 20
Jet Power 22
Land Yachts 24
Hovercraft 26
Notes for Parents and Teachers 28

Glossary 30
Books to Read 31
Index 32

AIR IS EVERYWHERE

Air is all around us. We cannot see it or feel it, but we know it is there. Without air there would be no animals or plants. When we breathe in air, our bodies use some of it to keep us alive.

Look at these people on a boat. Their hair is being blown by the wind.

Finding out that air is there

When the wind is blowing, it is really large amounts of air moving from place to place.

Go outside on a windy day. Try running against the wind. Is it quite difficult? Hold a large piece of cardboard in front of you as you run. Does this make it more difficult?

Make a chart of the wind. Every day, look to see how windy it is and make a note of it on your chart. There might be just a light **breeze**, or there might be a **gale** or **storm**. Look for signs of the wind like this:

	Flags hanging straight down	Calm
	Washing flapping	A breeze
	Trees swaying, twigs broken off	A gale
	Trees blown down	A storm

WINDMILLS

We can use air in many ways. The wind can be used to drive windmills or push boats along on the water. Modern windmills are used to make **electricity**.

This is a 'wind farm' where electricity is made.

Making a model windmill

You will need:

A cardboard box
Felt-tip pens
Some card
A paper fastener
Scissors

1. Draw a windmill on the box with felt-tip pens.

2. Cut out two strips of card for the **sails**.

3. Fix the sails on to the windmill with the paper fastener.

STARTING TECHNOLOGY

HAND WINDMILLS

Making a hand windmill

You will need:

- Stiff paper
- A pencil and ruler
- Scissors
- A strong pin
- A plastic bead
- A wooden stick

1. Cut out a square of paper and draw lines diagonally across it, from corner to corner.

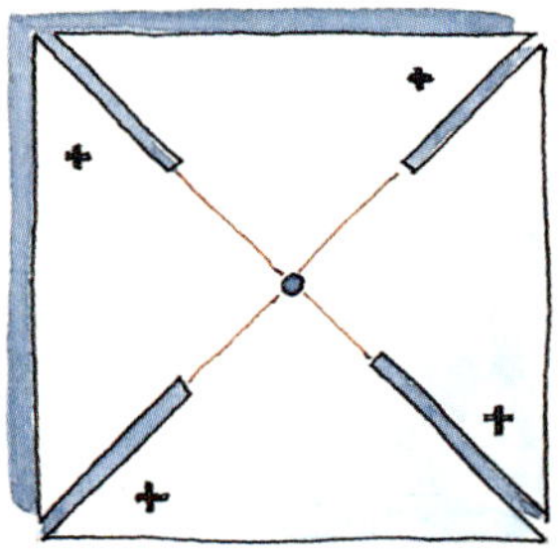

2. Make a small hole in the middle. Cut along the lines from each corner, half-way towards the middle.

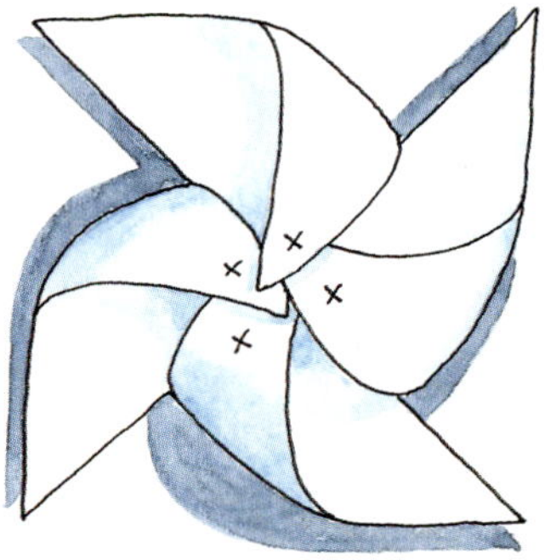

3. Fold the corners marked with a cross into the middle.

4. Stick the pin through each corner and then through the hole in the middle of the square. Put the pin through the bead and then fix it to the stick. Now try your windmill outside.

Further work

Try your hand windmill outside on different days. Make a chart to work out which is the best wind strength for your windmill. On different days, count how many times the windmill turns round in one minute. Colour one of the sails red to help you count them as they go round.

DAY	WIND STRENGTH	NUMBER OF TURNS	COMMENTS
Monday	Calm	None	Not moving
Tuesday	Breeze	Lots	Spinning fast
Wednesday	Light breeze	A few	Spinning quite fast

This hand windmill is just like the one you can make, except that it has more sails. Try to make one like this, using two pieces of card, one on top of the other.

WIND WHEELS

Making a wind wheel

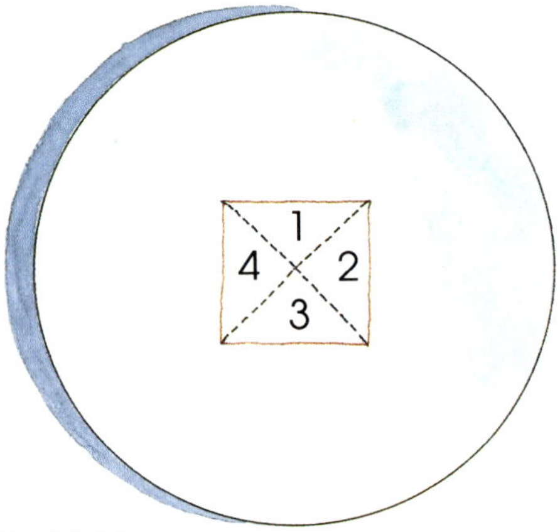

You will need:

A large piece of thick card
A plate
A pencil and ruler
Scissors

1. Draw a large circle, about 25 cm across, on the piece of card and cut it out. You will need a plate to draw round.

2. Draw a square in the middle of the circle. The sides of the square should be about 5 cm long.

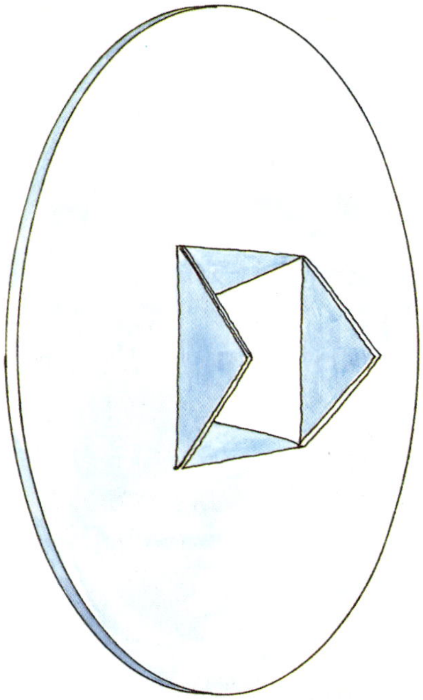

3. Draw a dotted line joining opposite corners of the square. Cut along these lines to make four triangles.

4. Fold the triangles numbered 1 and 3 out to one side of the wind wheel. Fold the other two triangles out to the other side.

5. Take the wheel outside and hold it upright on the ground. When the wind blows, take your hand away and watch your wind wheel move.

Further work

Make lots of wind wheels with triangular flaps of different sizes. With your friends, race them against each other to see which ones work best.

Make a wind wheel with just one flap folded out on each side. Does it work?

Have you ever blown the seeds from a dandelion? The wind will blow the seeds further than you can. They are lighter than your wind wheel so they will float through the air a very long way.

STARTING TECHNOLOGY

WIND FORCE

The force of the wind can be very strong. It can push over trees, overturn cars and even blow down houses. It is often useful for us to **measure** how strong the wind is.

Looking at flags is a good way to see how strong the wind is. These flags are blowing in a strong wind.

Measuring wind force

You will need:

Pieces of garden cane
Strips of tissue paper
Strips of thicker paper and cloth
Pieces of string
Drawing pins

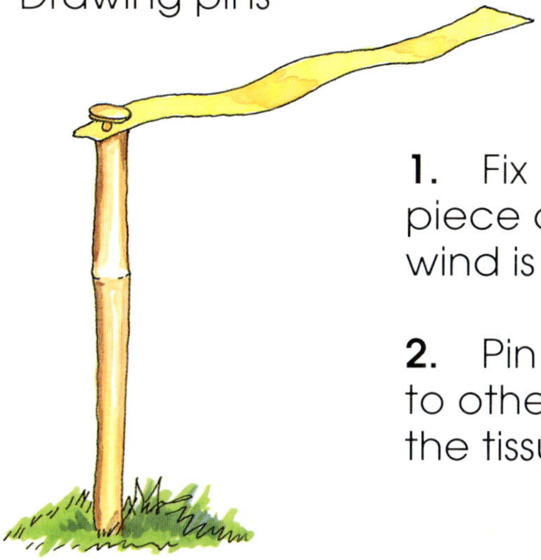

1. Fix a strip of tissue paper to the top of a piece of cane with a drawing pin. When the wind is blowing, the strip will blow straight out.

2. Pin strips of thicker paper, cloth and string to other canes. Do they blow out straight like the tissue paper?

3. Sort out the different strips of paper, cloth and string from lightest to heaviest.

MORE MEASURING

Making a machine for measuring wind force

You will need:

Two sticks of balsawood, about 30 cm long
A junior hacksaw
Wood glue
A piece of **dowel**
A plastic bottle
Four plastic cups
Strong pins

WARNING: Always ask an adult to help you cut balsawood.

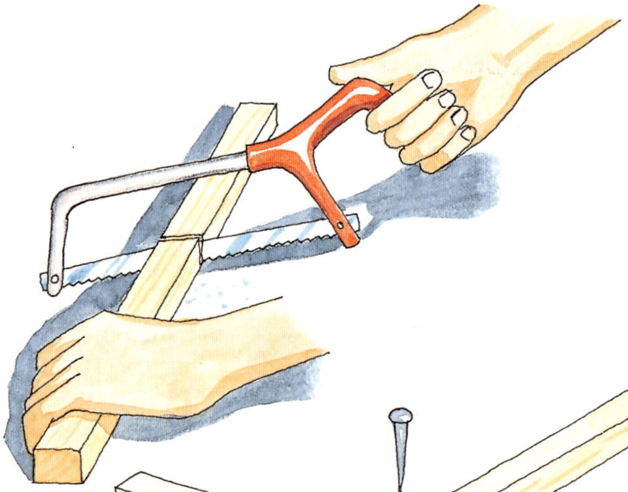

1. Cut a small piece out of the centre of each stick of balsawood with a hacksaw. Make sure you do not cut right through the wood.

2. Fit the pieces of balsawood together where you have made the cuts. Use a little glue.

3. Push a pin through the **joint** and into the end of the dowel. Use glue to fix it more firmly.

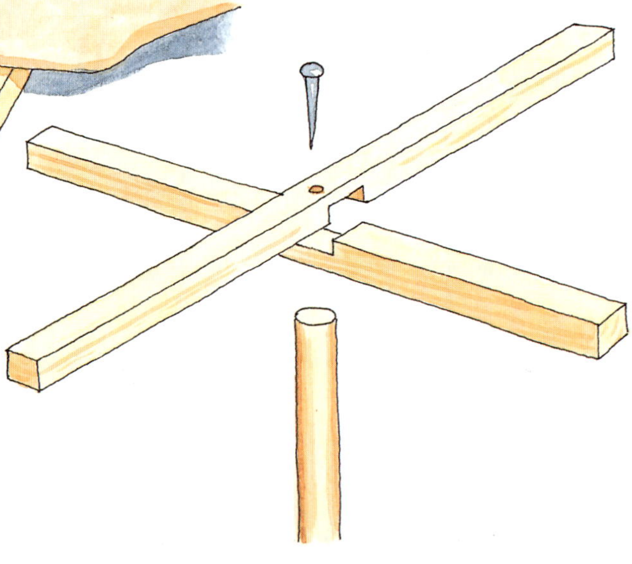

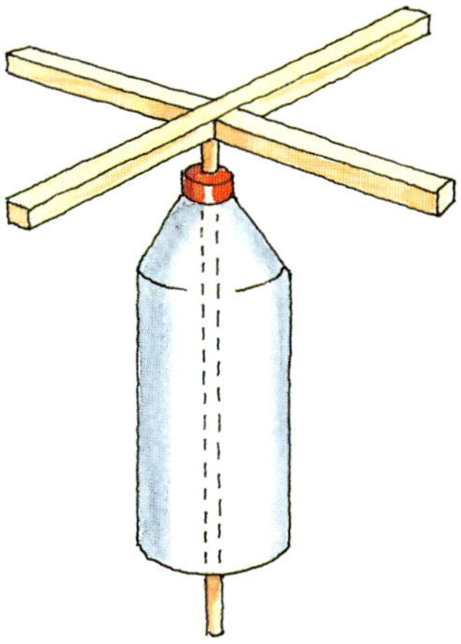

4. Make a hole in the bottom of the plastic bottle. Slide the dowel through the neck of the bottle, so that the end sticks out of the hole at the bottom.

5. Pin a plastic cup to the end of each balsawood arm. Make sure the cups all face in the same direction.

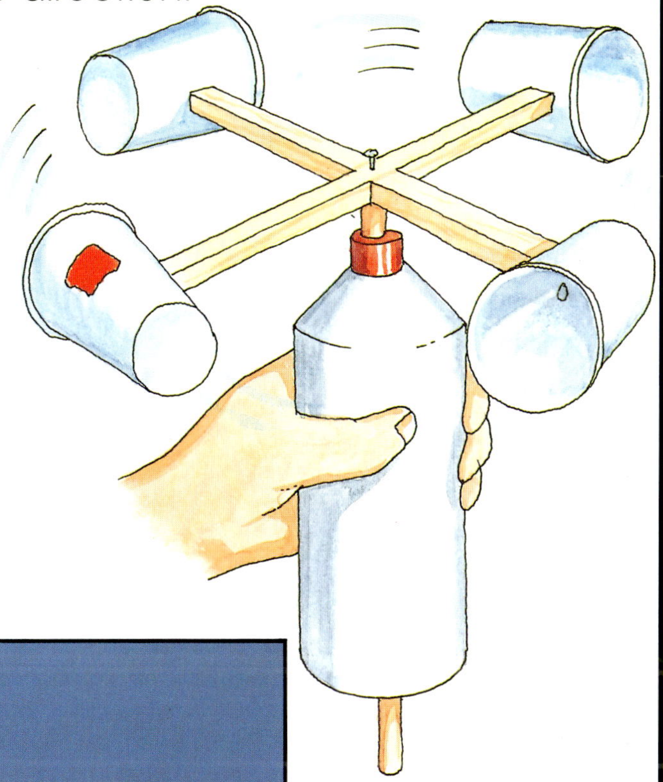

6. Hold your machine outside in the wind. Count how many times the cups go round in ten seconds. You can fix a coloured marker to one cup to help you count.

7. Take your machine out on another day and count again. Is the wind stronger or weaker than before?

These machines measure the force and direction of the wind.

KITES

Air can keep a **kite** flying. It can even keep a heavy aeroplane up in the sky. Have you ever flown a kite on a windy day?

Do you have a kite? This one is just like the kite you can make, only bigger. Look to see how the string is attached.

Making a mini kite for indoors

You will need:

Two drinking straws
Scissors
Cotton thread
Tissue paper
Paper glue
String

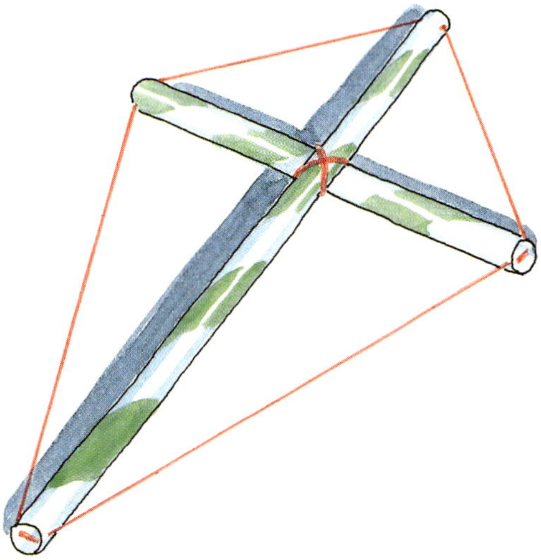

1. Cut the end off one of the straws to make it shorter. Tie the two straws in a cross shape with cotton and glue them together.

2. Join the four ends of the straws with cotton.

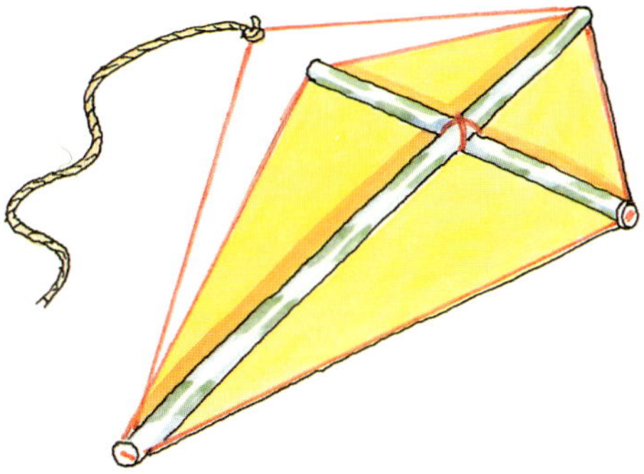

3. Cut out a piece of tissue paper in the shape of your kite. Glue it on to the straws and cotton.

4. Tie another piece of cotton to the top and bottom of the longest straw. Tie a piece of string to this thread.

5. To make a tail, tie lots of little pieces of tissue paper to a long piece of cotton. Attach this to the bottom of the kite.

6. In a large room, run along with the kite behind you, until you have let out all the string. You can also try the kite outside in a very light wind.

HOT-AIR BALLOONS

When air gets hot it rises upwards. This is how hot-air balloons work. The balloon is filled with hot air which lifts it off the ground and makes it fly.

There are lots of balloons in this picture. Can you see the people in the baskets?

Making a model hot-air balloon

You will need:

A party balloon
Tissue paper
Paper glue
Scissors
Paints
A matchbox
Cotton thread

1. Blow up the balloon and tie it so that the air does not come out.

2. Glue small pieces of tissue paper over the outside of the balloon. Cover most of it except the mouth end. Stick on several layers of paper and leave to dry.

3. When the balloon is hard, cut off the bottom of the balloon with scissors.

4. Paint and decorate your model. Hang the inside of the box underneath with cotton for the passenger basket.

5. Stick a piece of cotton to the top of the balloon so that you can hang it up.

PARACHUTES

Parachutes allow things to float gently down through the air. People can jump out of aeroplanes high in the sky if they have a parachute. The parachute allows them to float safely to the ground.

This is a special parachute. The man can steer it so that it lands in exactly the right place.

Making parachutes

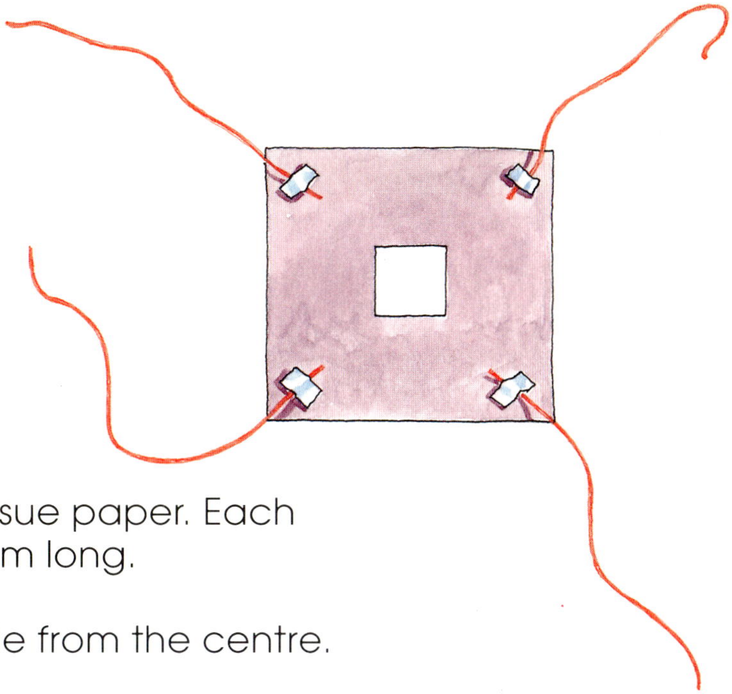

You will need:

Tissue paper
Scissors
Cotton thread
Sticky tape
A small lump of plasticine

1. Cut out a square of tissue paper. Each side should be about 30 cm long.

2. Cut a small square hole from the centre.

3. Fix pieces of cotton to each corner with sticky tape. Make sure all four pieces of cotton are the same length.

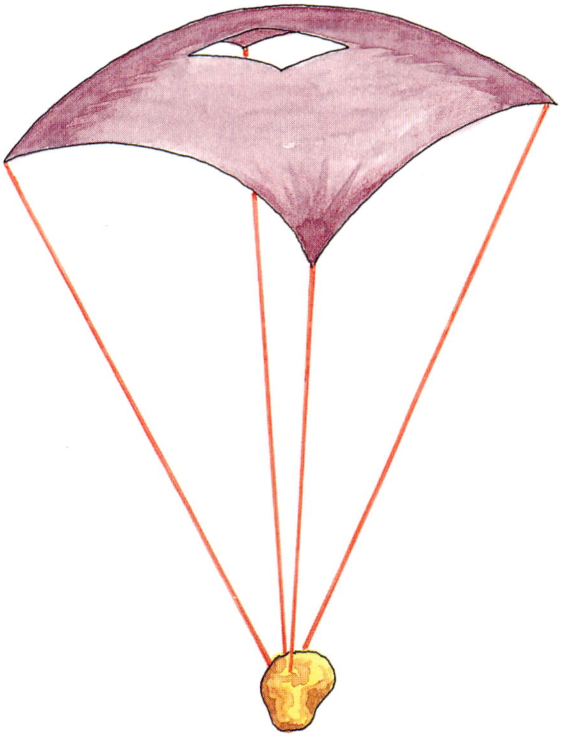

4. Attach the plasticine to the other ends of the threads.

5. Drop your parachute from as high as you can. Measure the time it takes for the parachute to reach the ground. **Do not climb on to ladders or chairs without an adult to help you.**

6. Make more parachutes. This time, cut several square holes out of the tissue paper. How many squares can you cut out before the parachute stops working?

STARTING TECHNOLOGY

JET POWER

Have you ever felt a **jet** of air? Blow up a balloon but do not tie the end. Hold the balloon and let the air out. Can you feel the air rushing out?

You have probably blown up balloons just like this. What happens when you let them go?

Making a balloon-powered racer

You will need:

Two strips of balsawood, one about 15 cm long and the other 10 cm long
Three wheels made from stiff card
A party balloon
A small piece of plastic tube
Sticky tape
Wood glue
Strong pins
Scissors

1. Fix the two pieces of balsawood together in the shape of a cross, using a pin and some glue.

2. Pin a wheel to either end of the short piece of wood. Pin the third wheel to one end of the other piece, at the side.

3. Cut the lip off the balloon. Stretch the open end over the plastic tube. Fix it tightly with sticky tape.

4. Attach the balloon and tube to the racer with more sticky tape.

5. Blow up the balloon, putting your finger over the end to stop the air coming out. Put your racer on the ground and let the air out.

LAND YACHTS

A land **yacht** is like a boat with a sail, but it has wheels and travels on land instead of water.

Making a land yacht

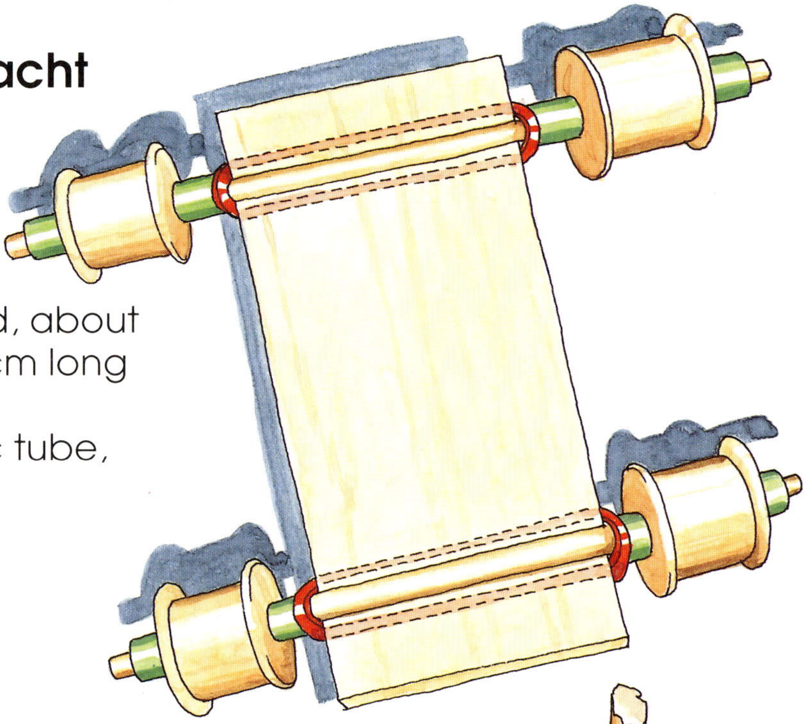

You will need:

Five cotton reels
A piece of balsawood, about 10 cm wide and 30 cm long
Garden canes
Small pieces of plastic tube, about 1 cm long
Rubber bands
Tissue paper
Cotton thread
Sticky tape
Scissors

1. Attach two garden canes across the piece of balsawood with rubber bands.

2. On each end of the canes, slide a cotton reel with pieces of plastic tube on either side. This is your trolley which will be the base of your yacht.

3. Fix another cotton reel in the centre of the trolley with two rubber bands.

4. Put a piece of garden cane into the hole in the middle of the cotton reel.

5. Cut out a sail from tissue paper in the shape of a triangle. Stick the top of the sail to the garden cane **mast** with a small piece of sticky tape.

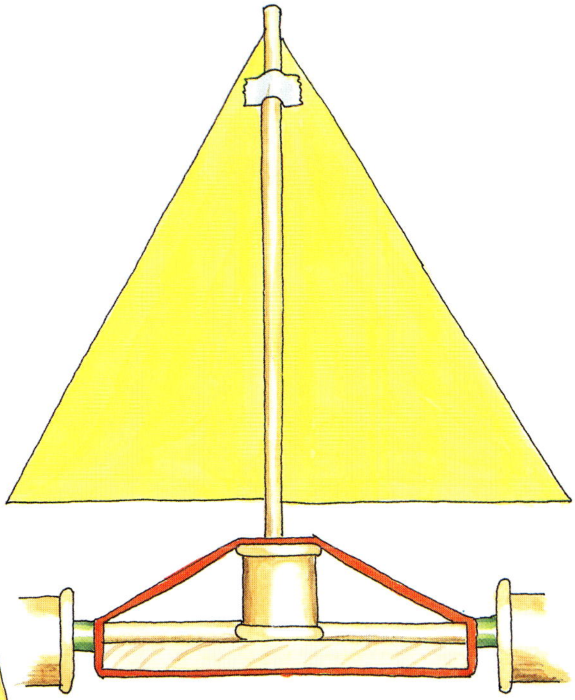

6. Stick two pieces of cotton thread to the other corners of the sail with tape. Tie the ends of the threads to the cane at the back of the yacht.

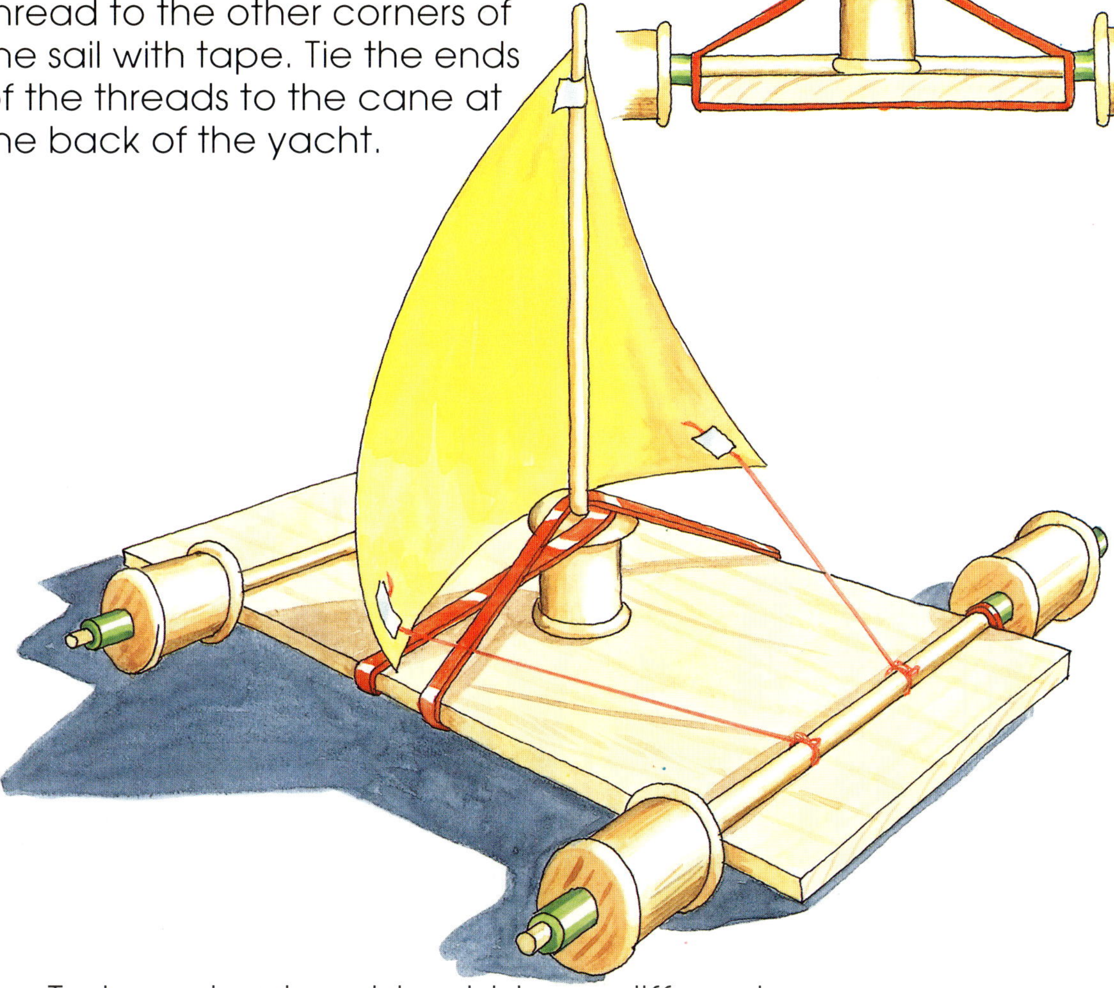

7. Test your land yacht outside on different days and in different strengths of wind.

HOVERCRAFT

Hovercraft look like big boats - but they are not boats at all! In fact, they travel just above the water on a kind of cushion of air. Hovercraft can also be used on dry land.

This big hovercraft can carry lots of people and cars.

Making a simple hovercraft

You will need:

A polystyrene tile
A small tube made of card
Four strips of card, 2 cm wide
Paper glue

1. Make a small hole in the centre of the tile.

2. Fit the tube of card tightly into the hole and fix it with a little glue.

3. Blow down the tube to see if the hovercraft will rise.

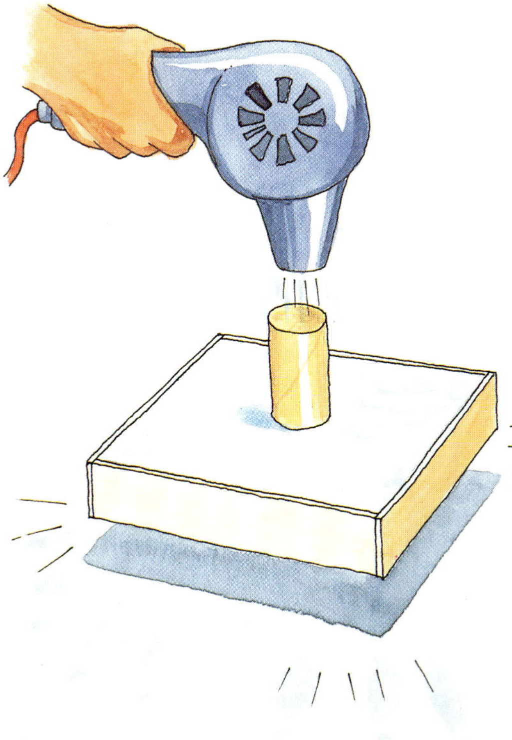

4. Stick the strips of card round the sides of the tile. Blow down the tube now. Can you make the hovercraft move along? You could ask an adult to use a hair drier to blow air down the tube.

WARNING:
Do not use a hair drier on your own. Always ask an adult to help you.

Notes for Parents and Teachers

SCIENCE AND TECHNOLOGY

Children may have studied the properties and importance of air in other topics. They may be aware that it is essential for life, but not realize its value in technology. Children should learn that air has substance. They can understand this by making models which need a 'solid' body of air to make them work.

Children should try to build these models with as little help from adults as possible. By doing much of the work themselves, children will become more aware of the materials used and understand better the science behind the technology. They will experience at first hand the forces and energy which make the models work.

All these models have actually been made by young children. Teachers should be able to judge how much help each individual child will need.

MATHEMATICS

Timing experiments and making records of wind force and vehicle speeds are all practical mathematical exercises. A practical approach to mathematics helps children come to terms with the use of numbers. They should be encouraged to be as accurate as possible, using a variety of devices, such as stop-watches, timers or their own pulse.

LANGUAGE

Language skills will develop from the activities in this book. Children will discuss among themselves how best to solve the various problems that arise. Most of this will go unrecorded. However, some written work will be involved. Descriptions of experiments and written results must be clear and concise, but children should also be allowed to use their imagination when writing about a model which they have built and made to work.

National Curriculum Attainment Targets

This book is relevant to the following Attainment Targets in the National Curriculum for science:

Attainment Target 1 (Exploration of science) The construction and testing of models throughout this book is relevant. Special attention should be paid to asking questions (level 2) and fair tests (level 3). The various methods of recording scientific work are included in this Attainment Target. Sections in this book on windy weather, hand windmills and measuring wind force involve recording findings as charts or pictures.

Attainment Target 9 (Earth and atmosphere) Finding out that air is all around us is included in this Attainment Target. Projects on wind, recording weather over a period of time and measuring wind force are also relevant.

Attainment Target 10 (Forces) Forces are involved in all the working models in this book which use the push of the wind or the force of gravity to make them move. Models with moving parts also involve friction.

Attainment Target 13 (Energy) All the moving models involve energy — kinetic or potential. Attention should be paid to the transfer of energy. For example, the movement of the wind is transferred to the movement of a land yacht by a sail.

The following Attainment Targets are included to a lesser extent:

Attainment Target 6 (Types and uses of materials) Children will need to experience the properties of different materials when choosing them for the various models.

Attainment Target 12 (Information technology) Children should be encouraged to record their work using computers.

Teachers should be aware of the Attainment Targets covered in other National Curriculum documents — that is, those for design and technology, mathematics, history and language.

GLOSSARY

Breeze A gentle wind.

Dowel A straight stick of solid wood.

Electricity Power that travels along wires. It is used for giving light and for making all sorts of machines work.

Gale A very strong wind.

Jet A thin stream of liquid or gas which is forced out of a small opening.

Joint The place where two parts fit together.

Kite A toy made of a light frame covered in paper or cloth. It is flown in the wind at the end of a piece of string.

Mast A tall pole which holds up the sail on a boat.

Measure To find out how big or heavy something is or how quickly it has moved.

Parachute A large piece of cloth that opens up when a cord is pulled, so that a person can jump out of an aeroplane and float safely to the ground.

Sails The parts of a windmill that are turned round by the wind. Sails are usually the pieces of strong cloth on a boat which catch the wind and make it move along.

Storm A very strong wind with a lot of rain or snow.

Yacht A sailing boat that can travel very quickly.

BOOKS TO READ

Air by Terry Jennings (Oxford University Press, 1982)
Air by Brenda Walpole (Kingfisher, 1987)
Air by Angela Webb (Franklin Watts, 1986)
Air in Action by Robin Kerrod (Cherrytree, 1988)
Amazing Air by Henry Smith (Methuen, 1982)
In the Air by Graham Weston (Wayland, 1983)
It's Windy by Laurie Bolwell (Wayland, 1985)
Wind Play by Ed Catherall (Wayland, 1986)

Picture acknowledgements
The publishers would like to thank the following for allowing their photographs to be reproduced in this book: Eye Ubiquitous 6, 18; Chris Fairclough Colour Library 11; Hutchison Library 4; Topham 26; Zefa 9, 12, 15, 16, 20, 22. Cover photography by Zul Mukhida.

INDEX

aeroplanes 16, 20

balloon-powered racers 23
balloons 18-19, 22-3
boats 4, 6, 24, 26
breathing 4
breezes 5, 9

calm 5, 9
charts 5, 9

dandelion seeds 11

electricity 6

flags 5, 12
flying 16, 18

gales 5

hand windmills 8-9
hot-air balloons 18-19
hovercraft 26-7

jet power 22-3

kites 16-17

land yachts 24-5

masts 25
mini kites 17

parachutes 20-21

sails 7, 9, 24-5
sky 16, 20
storms 5

trees 5, 12

wind 5-6, 9-17, 25
wind charts 5
wind force 12-15
windmills 6-9
wind wheels 10-11

yachts 24-5